WTF

summersdale

WTF

With research by Elanor Clarke.

Summersdale Publishers Ltd
46 West Street
Chichester
West Sussex
PO19 1RP
UK

www.summersdale.com

Printed and bound in China

ISBN: 978-1-84953-488-8

Substantial discounts on bulk quantities of Summersdale books are available to corporations, professional associations and other organisations. For details contact Nicky Douglas by telephone: +44 (0) 1243 756902, fax: +44 (0) 1243 786300 or email: nicky@summersdale.com.

INTRODUCTION

The Internet has given us millions of cute videos of puppies and kittens, but best of all, it has opened up a world of new words and phrases. We can use a 'hashtag' to comment amusingly on any situation, we can 'follow' people we like and 'retweet' the funny things they say, and we can utter an ever-so-polite 'WTF?!' when something outrages or shocks us.

From lethal coconuts to clued-up chihuahuas, and from a 400-year-old clam to a Christmas cracker as long as six London buses, this astonishing collection of baffling facts will provide food for thought even when you're in a Wi-Fi-free zone.

Rabbits are unable
to throw up.
#wishihadnteatenthat

On 16 December 1811, an earthquake caused some sections of the Mississippi River to flow backwards.
#bewaremoonwalkingrivers

#wtf

Starfish can turn their
stomachs inside out.
#starfishmumsdisapproveofthis

Bananas grow on shrubs, so there is no such thing as a banana tree.
#barkingupthewrongtree

Hawaii's state
fish is called the
humuhumunukunukuapua'a.
#bitofamouthful
#sorry?

Chameleons' tongues
are longer than
their bodies.
#usefulatbuffets

If you add all the numbers on a roulette wheel together, they total 666. #thedevilsgame

Donkeys kill more people each year than plane crashes.
#wheneeyoreturnsbad

WTF

In Pennsylvania, the funeral of a burger-loving 88-year-old man passed through his local drive-thru. Each mourner received a Whopper Jr burger. #canttakeitwithyou

It is physically impossible for a pig to look up into the sky.
#stayingdowntoearth
#nosetotheground

More people are killed by
coconuts than by sharks.
#ivegotadeadlybunchofcoconuts

An Ohio teacher took her
employers to court claiming
that she had a phobia of young
children.
#notinmyjobdescription

Albatrosses sleep whilst flying, to avoid predators.
#asleepatthewing

99 per cent of UK bank notes revealed traces of cocaine, according to a survey in 2000.
#itsjustacoldithink
#sniff

#wtf

Of all dogs, the chihuahua
has the largest brain
proportional to its body.
#bigbraintrappedinasmalldog
#toosmarttobehave?

#WTF

Sahara is an Arabic word which means 'desert', so saying 'Sahara desert' is like saying 'desert desert'.
#whatshallwecallit?
#howaboutdesert

Clint Eastwood was offered the roles of James Bond and Superman, and he turned them both down. #askyourself:doeshefeellucky?

We are mostly empty
space. If our atoms lost
all the empty space in
them, we would shrink
enough to fit into a cube
1/500th of a centimetre
on each side.
#smallisbeautiful

A day on Mercury lasts
longer than a year there.
#happynewyear!
#goodnight

Around half of the population has eyelash mites – tiny, nearly see-through mites that eat dead skin and oil around the base of lashes and eyebrow hairs.
#youarenotalone

Every letter in the word 'typewriter' is found in one row of a standard keyboard.
#evenonacomputer

Octopi have tastebuds all along their tentacles.
#newmeaningtofeelingfunny

A shrimp's head contains its heart.
#thoughtsoflove
#thinkwithyourheart

The most expensive domain name ever was sold for $13 million: sex.com. #wheretheresmucktheresbrass

The barreleye fish has
a see-through head,
and spends most of
its time with its eyes
swivelled upwards,
looking for prey.
#totallyclearheaded

It is possible for hot water to freeze faster than cold water; this is called the Mpemba effect. #hellcouldfreezeover

#wtf

Purple dye used to be
made from sea snail mucus.
#howdidtheyfindthatout

Ostriches are unable to
fly, but they can swim.
#notaseabirdhonest

Trained pigeons were used to carry secret messages across enemy lines during World War Two. #fasterthansnailmail

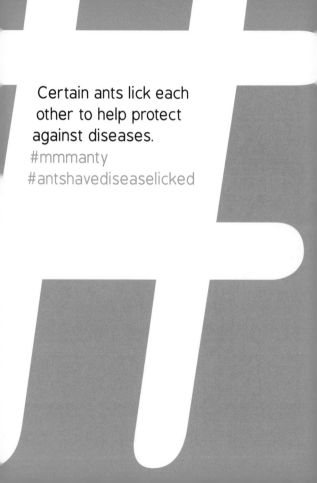

Certain ants lick each
other to help protect
against diseases.
#mmmanty
#antshavediseaselicked

The province of Newfoundland in Canada has its own time zone, 30 minutes behind Atlantic Standard Time. #outofstateoutoftime #theresalwaysone

Elvis Presley never played a concert in the UK. His only visit to the country was an hour spent in Prestwick airport in 1960. #sadtimesforBritain

Your body produces
about a litre of mucus
every day.
#snotpolite

Certain animals, including some frogs, are able to freeze solid in winter, then defrost in the spring and be perfectly healthy. #frogicicleanyone?

Frank and Louie are one cat with two faces. He is in the *Guinness World Records* as the longest surviving Janus cat.
#somecatsarejustsotwofaced

Your heart produces enough pressure to squirt blood 30 feet. #horrormovies:morerealisticthanyouthink

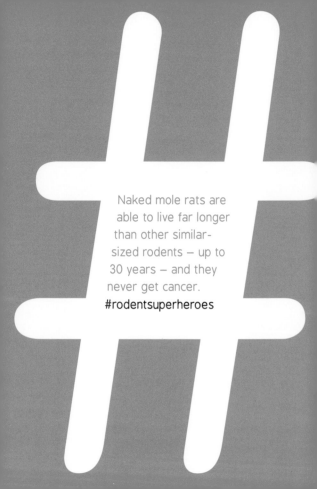

Naked mole rats are able to live far longer than other similar-sized rodents — up to 30 years — and they never get cancer.
#rodentsuperheroes

There is a species of
bacteria which can make
tiny nuggets of gold.
#truemeaningofgoodbacteria

John Cassidy holds the record for most balloon models made in one minute – 13.
#greatatbirthdayparties

#WTF

Kishan Valaiah Ayula of India swallowed 22 swords at once to earn a spot in the *Guinness World Records*.
#theressomethinginmythroat
#donttrythisathome!

The largest ball of cling film ever made had a circumference of 138 in, and weighed over 280 lb!

#thatcouldwrapalotofcheese

Cows with names
produce more milk
than nameless cows.
#godaisygo

Gerold Weschenmoser of Starzach in Germany holds the largest collection of masks in the world.
He even has one of his own face!
#amanofmanyfaces

Owls have three
sets of eyelids.
#areyouwinkingatme
#maybemaybemaybe

Lions have been known
to mate fifty times
in one day.
#toomuchofagoodthing?

Until the 1800s, there was no differentiation between left shoes and right, they were all straight.
#owmyfeetarekillingme!

Dalmatians are born completely white, and get their spots as they grow into adulthood.
#dogscanchangetheirspots

Lisa Courtney of Welwyn Garden City owns the largest collection of Pokemon memorabilia in the world, nearly 14,500 items. #ocp=obsessivecompulsive pokemon

There are 464 different
definitions for the
English word 'set', more
than any other word in
the English language.
#setsetandset
#asetofsetsatsunset

All Pixar characters blink just one eye at a time.
#blinkingorwinking?

#wtf

Viagra stops flowers from wilting. Among other things. #itsformygardenhonest!

#WTF

Rabbits are able to see behind themselves without turning their heads.
#360vision
#hideandseekinstantwin

Phobophobia is the word for a fear of phobias.
#catch22
#scaredofyourownfear?

Whale milk contains
more than
50 per cent fat.
#notgoodfordieters

It can take a whole week to make a jelly bean.
#andallforasecondoftaste

In *The Godfather*, every time someone dies there are oranges in the room.
#orangesarethedeadliestfruit

Amongst those accused
of stealing the 'Mona Lisa'
was Pablo Picasso.
#artistturnsartthief?

Ducks have more bones in their necks than giraffes.
#specquackular

Ukulele means 'jumping flea', coined because of the way the player's fingers move across the strings.
#orbecauseitplingsandpings
#dofleassoundlikeukuleles?

The first commercial Frisbees were actually called 'Pluto Platters'. #wouldntsaturnmakemoresense?

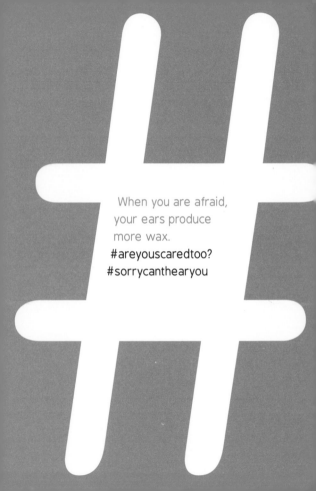

When you are afraid,
your ears produce
more wax.
#areyouscaredtoo?
#sorrycanthearyou

If you kept your pet goldfish in the dark, it would lose its pigment and become white. #alwaysbelieve:youaregold!

If a deep sea diver's pump failed, all that would be left inside their suit would be their skeleton.
#deepseadanger
#skeletoncrew

#WTF

A bat's leg bones are so thin that they are unable to walk, otherwise their legs would break. #goodthingtheyhavewings

#WTF

There is such a thing as fear of food, it is called sitophobia. #nothanksimfull

Kissing can cause tooth decay due to the bacteria in saliva.
#worththerisk

Male bees die after mating.
#nottonightjosephine

Buzz Lightyear was
originally called
'Lunar Larry'.
#tothemoonandbeyond?

It is possible for pigs to become alcoholics and, like many animals, they enjoy eating fermented fruits.

#drunkasapig

Killer whales are actually
a kind of dolphin.
#killerdolphindoesntsoundright

A 'jiffy' is actually a specific length of time, not just a phrase.
#andapostagebag
#inajiffymorespecificthanyouthought

Leeches have 34 'brains', though none of these is a complete brain. #doesthatmakethemsmarterthanpeople?

Scientists have genetically altered a goat so that it produces spider silk in its milk. #spidergoat!

The potoo bird camouflages itself as a tree to hide from both predators and prey.
#cantseethebirdforthetrees

#wtf

Captain Kirk's famous phrase, 'Beam me up, Scotty', was actually never said on *Star Trek*. #thoughscottydidbeamhimup

#WTF

Robert Chesbrough, the inventor of Vaseline, claimed he ate a spoonful of it every day.
#justslidesdown
#welloileddigestivemachine

Bananas are naturally
slightly radioactive.
#thatswhyericisbananaman

A human head has
the same density
as a watermelon.
#notastastythough

Australia is home to twice as many kangaroos as people.
#mustmakethemhoppingmad

According to colour psychology, the colour red makes you feel hungry. #notifitsredmashedpotatoes

There are 17 countries
smaller than Florida's
Disney World.
#largerthanlife

Although they live their lives in water, whales will drown if they do not come up for air.
#makesiteasiertospotthem

WTF

Though many people lost their lives when the *Titanic* sank, among the saved were five dogs and a pig.
#womenchildrenandanimalsfirst

Some penguins are prostitutes.
They use sex to get rocks for
their nests.
#getyourrockson

Mosquitos are thought to be more attracted to people who have recently eaten bananas. **#theygobananasforfruit**

Broccoli is not just a vegetable, it is also a flower. If left for a long time the green flower buds will open out to yellow flowers.
#sayitwithbroccoli

#wtf

The largest Christmas cracker in the world had a diameter of four metres and was 63 metres long. #bigbang

#WTF

The strawberry is the only fruit
with its seeds on the outside. It is
also not a berry. But a banana is.
#worldview:destroyed

If you decided to feed it one, a Venus flytrap could digest a cheeseburger.
#omnomnomnom
#hecanhazcheezburger

Elephants are excellent swimmers, and have been known to swim up to 30 miles in one go.
#elepaddle

A woman from Spain has legal ownership of the sun.
#askpermissionbeforeusing

The oldest known animal
is a 405–410-year-old
clam named Ming.
#mingtheendless
#toughasoldboots

If you're interested in finding out
more about our books,
find us on Facebook at
Summersdale Publishers
and follow us on Twitter at
@Summersdale.

www.summersdale.com